THE
NEXT RIGHT THING
SIMPLE PRINCIPLES, EXTRAORDINARY RESULTS!

BRANDON ANSEL

CLEARFOCUS PRESS

The Next Right Thing – Simple Principles, Extraordinary Results

Brandon Ansel

Copyright © 2013 Brandon Ansel

Published in the United States by ClearFocus Press

ISBN: 0615852394

ISBN 13: 9780615852393

CONTENTS

Preface

First of all, *thank you* for taking the time to read this book!

As it turns out, the first person to read this little project was my mother, and she said it was great, so I am, no doubt, expecting rave reviews due to her unbiased, expert opinion on literary genius. ☺

That being said, I hope you will read this book with an open mind and spirit. I also hope that you will not let the fact that I am, currently, not a wealthy, successful, $50 million man drown out or invalidate the truths that I've observed and written about in these chapters.

I am exactly where I am supposed to be in my personal journey, and, candidly, I feel like a multibillionaire when wealth is measured in joy, peace, excitement, and fulfillment in this life.

This book is certainly an important piece to the puzzle for me as I work hard toward my personal and family goals. I trust that as you meditate on its incredibly simple yet profound truths, and sometimes-funny stories, you will be inspired to constantly engage The Next Right Things in your life journey toward the future that you envision and claim for yourself!

I also believe it is important to let you know that I fully recognize that I have probably not said anything in this book that has not already been said before in some way, shape, or form. My purpose in writing the way that I did was to offer an easy-to-read idea map for myself and for anyone else who picks up the book. My hope is that you find that the text can be very simply referenced or reread when appropriate.

It would be an incredible honor if, after reading this book, you would take the time to send me an e-mail and let me know some of The Next Right Things that are impacting your world or the world around you. Let me know what I've missed too! I have no less than fifteen other chapters/stories/truths that I've learned from or observed through writing these words...maybe I should have included some of them, I don't know.

Blessings on your day!

-Brandon Ansel
brandonansel@gmail.com
www.brandonansel.com
Spring Arbor, Michigan
June 24, 2013

CHAPTER ONE

THE NEXT RIGHT THING

"Talking is easy, action is difficult."

– Spanish Proverb

It is 11:25 a.m. on Saturday, May 11, 2013, and for me, The Next Right Thing to do is to sit down and write this book. If you are reading this book, chances are you have extremely big goals and dreams that you fully intend to accomplish. You bought this book to, hopefully, find some wisdom to help you fulfill your destiny. Well, listen up, because reading this book is, without doubt, The Next Right Thing, and I'm going to spend the next several hours and several hundred pages defining what that means for me, how difficult it is to actually do The Next Right Thing, and giving you the tools to embrace this life principle for your personal health and wealth.

In the book *The Secret*, by Rhonda Byrne, the co-creator of the *Chicken Soup for the Soul* book series,

Jack Canfield, provides a cool analogy: when driving at night from California to New York, you don't need to see all the way from one coast to another. All you need is for your headlights to show you the next two hundred feet in front of you, and you will get there. In life, you have to trust that you will be shown the way. Most people, he observes, never ask for what they want because they cannot see *how* it could possibly come to them.

As a young guy with lofty goals and dreams, I often feel in my soul what Canfield is talking about, and The Next Right Thing is what guides me through my days.

I have a very clear vision of where I'm heading in life, in business, in my marriage and relationships, etc. Often, though, I feel like I am on a journey, driving in the dark, fully aware that my destination is out there...but without a map. I also realize that there are any number of routes to my destination, with truly no best route. My headlights are only shining out two hundred feet in front of me, showing me the potential twists and turns along my journey, illuminating all sorts of potentially exciting and interesting distractions along the way. The only true north that I have in this entirely complex journey that we call existence is to try to center myself every day, and in every moment be able to ask myself the following question:

"What is The Next Right Thing you should be doing, Brandon Ansel, to propel you toward your goals while enjoying peace and fulfillment in this moment?"

The problem is that the above question is easy to ask, but extremely complex to answer day in and day out.

This is truest when you own your own business *and* have a family. The answer to the question can literally change in a moment's notice. If you have a family and are in any type of business environment, you know exactly what I mean.

One second you are enjoying listening to your beautiful oldest daughter rehearse for her piano recital, the next second your cell phone is ringing, and you grab your phone to silence it but notice the call is from a potential client that you've been trying to work with. You now have an important choice to make. Depending on how much time you get to spend with your children, The Next Right Thing may be to ignore the call and give your daughter your full attention. On the other hand, if you've been listening for an hour, and you really need this new client, The Next Right Thing may be to sneak into your home office and take the call. Only you know which move is the next right step, and only you can choose accordingly.

As a personal and perfect example of this, I just received an e-mail from one Steve Carlson, a gentleman whom I've done work for in the past. Mr. Carlson has chosen to take time out of his busy Saturday (he owns restaurants) to refer a potential new client to me. The fork in the road is that I have desired to sit down and start this book for several years now, and for some unknown reason, today it has happened. If I stop typing now, while the words are flowing and my fingers are moving quickly, who knows when The Next Right Thing will be to sit down and put words on paper (or this computer screen). All I can do is trust my instincts, save this document, and respond to the e-mail from Mr. Carlson.

I'm back, and the e-mail from Steve actually led to a meeting at one of his restaurants. It was absolutely the right thing to get with Steve and learn about the opportunities he is suggesting that I pursue! Even if the time with Steve had not led to a unique business opportunity, by dropping everything and giving him my attention, I honored our relationship. Ultimately, relationships are the cornerstone of everything in business and in life!

ACTION ITEMS:

- I firmly believe that you intuitively always know The Next Right Thing to do. The trick is being tuned in to that inner voice that will guide you, and immediately focusing your attention to accomplish a task or do something meaningful!

- Keep reading, you will not regret it! But if you do end up hating the book, give me a call, 517.795.4850, and you can tell me to pound sand. ☺

CHAPTER TWO

WHO THIS BOOK IS FOR

"There is nothing to writing. All you do
is sit down at a typewriter and bleed."

—*Ernest Hemingway*

In 2008 I started blogging in an attempt to organize my thoughts and stop them from swirling around in my head. It is hard to get a good night's sleep when interesting ideas are poking at you all night! As a young businessman in my late twenties, I felt like there was very little practical information out there to help me be successful in life. I had read nearly every popular book by wealthy, successful people who were telling me how to become wealthy and successful. Very little rang true. What I wasn't getting from these authors was actionable advice that a guy with big dreams, but few resources, could start executing immediately to further his journey toward peace and prosperity.

That blog, *The Almost Millionaire* (thealmostmillionaire.com), was my attempt to find order and action out of the chaos of my thoughts and dreams.

The fact is, the blog is horrible, and there is probably very little of value there for anyone but me. But for me, the value was immeasurable. It got me in the habit of getting ideas out of my mind and on paper. This is hugely important! I believe that those nagging thoughts or ideas that keep you up at night are very important in obtaining your personal goals. They are like having the author of all knowledge, and your consciousness, plotting together and pushing you toward your destiny. *Don't ignore them!* Get them on paper and give them the attention that they deserve. If something is constantly on your mind, it is probably important, and most likely unresolved. Resolution is one of the most powerful forces for good in the universe! Resolution leads to action, which leads to peace, health, and wealth.

So if you are like me and you started your first business with nothing more than a strong work ethic and $20,000 in cash advances from your credit cards, *this book is for you*.

My prayer is that you walk away from these words with a laundry list of potential Next Right Things that you can act on immediately to better your world and the world around you. My first bit of advice is to get your thoughts out of your head and on paper, whether you plan on ever writing a book or not! Remember, resolution leads to action, which leads to peace, health, and wealth.

- Have you ever observed a successful athlete who wasn't constantly taking action to better his game?

- Do you know an impactful preacher who doesn't relentlessly study the Good Book?

- Are there top sales professionals out there who aren't constantly pawing at the earth to uncover the next deal?

- Try to find me a successful entrepreneur who isn't passionate about his or her business...I'll bet you can't!

- Have you met many couples forty years into marriage who aren't doing the little things to love on their spouse? I doubt it!

Action Items:

- Use your smartphone "Notes" app, a scratch pad, or the pages of this book, to get those ideas/concepts/revelations out of your head and organized into items you can resolve to take action on. You will know instinctively which items are worth pursuing and which are just background noise. Focus you attention on things you are passionate about!

- With your more interesting notes, start a blog! Focus on sharing your unique ideas or knowledge with the world. This can be about anything: craft beer, homeschooling, raising chickens, gourmet coffee, accounting spreadsheets...whatever floats your boat. You will be surprised at how many folks are out there looking for unique perspectives like yours!

- *Take action* on the cool idea that starts rising to the top of the pile! Commit to do one little thing every day to bring your idea to the world.

- Start thinking like an entrepreneur. Learn from those who have gone before you! Pick up books by Timothy Ferriss, Guy Kawasaki, and

Pat Flynn to get your mind moving in the right direction. Jack Welch is a great businessman, no doubt, but his work provided me with little insight on how to start something from scratch.

CHAPTER THREE

START WITH THE END IN MIND

"I can't change the direction of the wind,
but I can adjust my sails to always reach
my destination."

—*Jimmy Dean*

In April 2003, my partner and I had just borrowed approximately $100,000 to open our first franchised pizza business together. I was extremely excited, yet harbored a healthy amount of fear. I had just turned twenty-four years old, and at the time that debt seemed like a burden, not the hardworking friend and money machine it would turn out to be...more on debt later!

Anyway, after a very long day of learning the pizza business at a training store in Swanton, Ohio, my partner and I were driving back to Jackson, Michigan, plotting the success of our new business venture. I remember it like it was yesterday. That was the first time The Next Right Thing slapped me in the face.

The Next Right Thing, in that moment, was to create the future with our words and get our vision on paper for the first time. I looked at my partner and said, "Let's write down our life goals, so we can compare where we are in ten years!" He loved the idea, and that is what we did!

I can't remember what he wrote down, but I know exactly where my mind was that beautiful spring day, mostly because I have kept that little piece of paper folded up in my wallet for the past ten years so I can easily read and remember it:

> Personal goal, $1,000,000 net worth by age thirty-five,
> $1,000,000 liquid by age FORTY, with great family lives!

Over the past ten years I've had the privilege of observing several great leaders creating the future with their thoughts and words. I believe that thoughts are things, and we make them real in our lives by speaking them or writing them down and claiming the future that we want for ourselves.

I have been overwhelmingly blessed over the past ten years and wake up every morning excited to attack and embrace the new challenges and opportunities of the day! That being said, when I think back to that drive home from Swanton, Ohio, in 2003, I can't help but think that *I should have dreamed bigger and should have taken the time to write down more important things*:

- How many more wells could have been dug for clean water in Africa?

- How many more meals could have been served at the Interfaith Shelter?

- How many more kids could I have mentored?

- How many more business opportunities could have been pursued?

I recognize that the past is the past, and it is what it is...but I've learned from the past and I hope you will too! Dream big, get it down on paper, take action, have fun, and make it real!

I took my seven-year-old daughter on a date last night. While we were driving to the restaurant, she asked me, "Daddy, you know when you blow on those white puffy flowers and make a wish...has one of those wishes ever come true for you?" I smiled big and glanced back at her sweet little face with the deep dimple under her left eye and said, "Emersyn, I'm going to tell you a secret. *All* of Daddy's wishes have come true, and yours can too!"

Jeremiah 29:11 (New International Version): "For I know the plans I have for you," declares the Lord, "plans to prosper you and not to harm you, plans to give you hope and a future."

I give you the verse above, simply because as I wrote the paragraph above, it hit me. I hope it gives you peace and hope in your personal journey, as it has for me!

That is what I mean by starting with the end in mind. There is nothing simpler than this!

If you don't know where you are going, how are you going to get there?

Action Items:

- Create a road map for your life's goals and define what you are capable of achieving. Focus on family, faith, business, or other things you are passionate about.

- Look at your road map every morning, tape it on the bathroom mirror, and use it as a guide for how to invest your time and efforts. This can be as complex as you like, or as simple as a Post-it note folded in your wallet.

- Believe!

- Don't be afraid to adjust your sails based on the direction that your life's wind is blowing.

CHAPTER FOUR

TIME

"To conquer frustration, one must remain intensely focused on the outcome, not the obstacles."

—*T. F. Hodge*

I have named this chapter "Time," but the fact is that I want to convey the power of intense focus, especially as it relates to time. I'm a little embarrassed to admit that I've wanted to write this book for over six years. Time is money, as they say, and The Next Right Thing, it appears, has been to focus on my business and family endeavors over the past six years...not to write a book.

The crazy thing is this: I suspect that I'm going to have a total of forty hours, one workweek, into the actual writing of this book. It has happened pretty darn quickly now that I've given it focus! I totally wish I had understood the power of *intense focus* years ago, because if I had, I would have passed out *a lot* of books as Christmas presents to family and friends over the past six years! (Hooray, another copy of Brandon's book, just what I wanted for Christmas, again. ☺)

If you have ever tried to drive and text message at the same time, *don't ever do that again!* Life is too short and every day is a gift! But if you have tried that crazy game of chicken with death, you probably realized, quickly, how bad the human brain is at doing two totally different things well at the same time.

There are all sorts of great books about brainpower out there. Everything I have ever read concludes that the human brain works at optimal capacity only when *intensely focused* on one thing (that thing, hopefully, being The Next Right Thing). You are making a huge mistake, in business and in life, if you don't learn how to do one thing really well at a time.

I am not saying you should not diversify your business ventures or invest in several friendships/relationships over the course of your life—quite the opposite, actually. I love the concept of taking your love, passions, and talent in several directions...just not at the same time. Of the seven business ventures I'm involved with, I give each of them a level of intense focus every day, based on the needs of each and what I believe is The Next Right Thing that I can do to push an individual project or business forward!

There is a very interesting verse in the Bible about the fact that no person is able to serve two masters. Here it is:

"No one can serve two masters. Either you will hate the one and love the other, or you will be devoted to the one and despise the other. You cannot serve both God and money." Matthew 6:24 (NIV)

> "No one can serve two masters..."
>
> "You cannot serve both God and money."

This wise proverb could not be truer in the context of *intense focus*. When you set yourself to the accomplishment of a goal that is extremely important to you, it can consume you and, in a sense, become your master. You will never serve a good master with the care and attention a good master expects and deserves if you are multitasking and giving yourself to two goals at once. By being able to *intensely focus* on the task at hand, the good master of that moment, you give yourself the best shot at achieving your goal. There are few better feelings in life than achieving an important goal.

Money is important in a capitalist system of commerce, but it is *never* worth serving. In the book *How Much Is Enough? Money and the Good Life*, author Robert Skidelsky writes, "Making money cannot be an end in itself...at least for anyone not suffering from acute mental disorder. To say that my purpose in life is to make more and more money is like saying that my aim in eating is to get fatter and fatter" (p. 5).

I have met hundreds of financially wealthy people over the years. It is my opinion that *not even one* of them finds even 50 percent of his of her personal joy, happiness, and fulfillment in their money.

Truly successful people view money as nothing more than the fun measuring stick that it is.

If you're doing things that you love and are *intensely focused* on important goals, your money will go up. If you are trudging through the day without joy, but with a defeatist attitude, halfheartedly doing work that you despise, I can promise you, your money will go down.

This leads me to another truth. *Every moment in life is an intense, incalculably valuable gift!* I try to commit every moment I have to things that matter, that are valuable, important, and loved by me. I advise you to do the same; whatever it is that fills you with joy!

(Is another episode of *The Simpsons* really the best use of your Monday evening?)

Invest your time wisely! Do important things. Always fill your life with ever-increasing moments of love and joy. Tell your kids one more bedtime story. Kiss your spouse just a couple of seconds longer. Go the extra mile in preparing that presentation. Dole out that little bit of extra praise to your people for a job well done. Protect those driving around you and reply to that text message later. Make that one extra sales call. Hug your mom just a wee bit tighter. I'm sure by now you get the point I am trying to make: *invest your precious moments wisely!*

BE INTENTIONAL

In closing, my thoughts on time:

The secret of the sauce is committing your time to important things and being in the moment, truly in the moment, with the task at hand. As I type this, I am at a restaurant, it is loud, and I sense there is a lot going on in the background, but there is only one place my brain is at right now. It is right here with you, the one reading these words. It is a crazy skill to learn, but once you have mastered it, your personal productivity will go through the roof. You will shock yourself!

Action Items:

- Stop texting and driving. Life is too valuable. It is dangerous and stupid. There is plenty of *time* for these communications when you're not on the road. (For what it's worth, the reason I am harping on texting and driving so much is that I was nearly run off the road this morning on my way to the office by some business dude who was double thumbing his BlackBerry.)

- Cool gift idea: For her next birthday, give your kid a homemade coupon that she can redeem for a date night, whenever she wants. That *time* together will mean way more than another plastic toy or stuffed animal.

- Practice intense focus every chance you get. Make a game out of it. Try to be so intensely focused on an important task that you almost feel a little ridiculous. Don't be discouraged! It took me years for intense focus to become second nature.

- Gamble with your money, *not* with your time. You can always make more money; precious moments are a bit harder to get back. (Or don't gamble at all; the blackjack dealer *always* seems to pull a twenty-one when I'm dealt two queens. What a scam. ☺)

CHAPTER FIVE

WORK

"Talent is cheaper than table salt. What separates the talented individual from the successful one is a lot of hard work."

—*Stephen King*

"The only way to enjoy anything in this life is to earn it first."

—*Ginger Rogers*

My father has sold furniture for a living sixty-plus hours per week for the past thirty-four years. Evening and weekend work has *always* been a part of our family life. I have never known a time where my dad didn't simply get his butt out of bed, with a smile on his face, and get to work.

The furniture business can be backbreaking work. In his younger years, you would rarely find my father standing around, waiting for the next customer to walk through the door. When Mom would bring me to the store to visit Dad, he was always lifting a couch and moving it from here to there, trying to make the room collections more inviting to customers so he could sell more. After the sale, he always helped load the customer's purchase. He knew how to serve people well, which created repeat business and referral leads.

My father *loves* what he does to make a living! For twenty years of his career, in addition to his sixty-plus hours a week, he had a forty-five-minute drive each way. *I have no recollection of him ever complaining about his work.* He had rough days, for sure. Selling the public anything comes with its share of challenges—humans can be crazy sometimes. He always loved his work, though, and was thankful for the opportunity, every day, to provide the American dream for his family.

I understand that it has been said before, but it is true, important, and worth saying again:

> If you're doing something important, something you love, it will never feel like work.

This is truly the key to a great work life, and it bleeds over into a great marriage and relationships too!

It strikes me that I consistently work twelve-plus-hour days, but it *rarely* feels like a burden. It brings me *way* more joy to do productive, important things than any feeling of "work" that is involved...and I've been doing this for fifteen years.

If you've ever said to your spouse, "I can't believe that I get paid to do this, it is so much fun!," you are truly blessed and have found the magic key to a fulfilling career.

If you are not there yet, and many people are not, I offer you the following tips.

ACTION ITEMS:

- Write down the "perfect" job, career, or business endeavor that you are currently qualified for. Then write down the "perfect" job, career, or business endeavor that you may not be qualified for, but could be educated toward. The Next Right Thing most likely involves taking steps to land that new job or getting the education you may need to prepare you to do that which will bring you more joy.

- Hard work and common sense seem to be quite uncommon in the world that we live in. Embrace hard work and common sense and you will stand out, without doubt!

- Take responsibility for your current reality. No one but *you* has gotten you where you are right now, good or bad as your current situation may be. By taking responsibility, you give yourself the power to be proactive and start taking the steps to change your situation. If you're constantly blaming others, you will be stuck in an endless cycle wherever you are.

- Seek out others who can help you get to the next level in your career. Let your intentions be known. People respond well to people who know what they want and are not afraid to ask for it. Ambition is a good basic instinct!

- Give, give, give! My father's job description did not include loading up customer purchases or lifting heavy furniture...but he did!

- Work hard to find joy in your current situation. I'm not sure that my dad's dream job was ever the retail furniture business, but he found joy in every day, and his career just got better and better every year. He has a beautiful home, a cottage on the lake, a vacation home in Florida, and flexibility in his schedule. All those blessings, yet he never loses sight of the *hard work* that got him there. He has figured out a way to sell a million dollars a year in furniture in thirty hours a week, where it used to take him sixty. He may be working smarter, but he is still working hard!

CHAPTER SIX

EDUCATION

"Live as if you were to die tomorrow.
Learn as if you were to live forever."

—*Mahatma Gandhi*

So I didn't do very well in high school. The fact of the matter is that I was *way* too busy chasing around my future wife—my educational pursuits just couldn't measure up to her allure! I did get straight As one semester in eleventh grade, but only because my grandfather put a $500 carrot in front of me. Like most humans, I've always been a little "dollar signs" motivated.

I did end up going to college, and did well, but I almost gave up. I dropped out after my first year because the business world was calling my name.

In 1998 my Uncle Brett and my father opened a Mancino's Pizza and Grinder restaurant on Eureka Road in Wyandotte, Michigan. I like to say I was the "operating partner," but in reality I was the only person crazy enough to manage the store. I got up every morning at 4:30 a.m. I had to be at the store by 5:30 a.m. to start baking the bread...baking the bread...baking the bread. The grinder bread seemed to stack up endlessly, but it was good, honest work! The store closed at 11:00 p.m., and sixteen-hour days were quite normal for me, especially when we first opened up. There were several nights that I threw a sleeping bag on the ground and slept at the restaurant—saved me the forty-five-minute drive each way.

I was chief pizza maker, and I loved it! But it only lasted a year.

That year at Mancino's certainly changed my life, and I received one heck of a real-world education. The more significant life-changing experience, though, was the sage advice that I received from one of my freshman-year business professors, Professor Piper.

Professor Piper saw something in me that I apparently didn't see in myself. She had devised a plan where I could receive college credit for the work experience I was gaining at Mancino's. The caveat was that I had to come back to school after a year and finish my business degree.

Her message was this:

> *"You may be doing well managing a pizza business, but come back to school, get your education, and you will learn how to run an organization."*

God bless her! She was right, and it changed the trajectory of my life in a major way.

After resigning as chief pizza maker, I spent the next two years busting through the business administration program at Spring Arbor University as fast as I possibly could. I learned to love the educational aspects of college, but truly wanted to get this "organizational knowledge" as fast as I could, so I could get my butt back into the business world.

There are definitely two sides to the higher education equation. We have all heard the stories of college dropouts who follow their dreams and go on to be wildly successful. I have also read articles that used quantitative data to show that sometimes it makes better financial sense to not spend $100,000 on schooling but to head straight for the work force instead.

For me, education truly made all the difference, and I would advise anyone with big business aspirations to give college a chance. Knowing what you know is good, but there is *great power* in knowing what you *don't* know! I thought I was pretty smart and doing a great job running that pizza store, but I thank God on a regular basis for the wisdom that caused me to listen to my professor, who knew *way* more about business than I did.

Professor Piper helped me understand that for me, education was, no doubt, The Next Right Thing. She helped create my future with her words...it is amazing how great leaders can do that! By 2005 I was *running* an organization consisting of five restaurants, doing a couple of million in annual sales, with over one hundred employees. I was working hard, but was working *way* fewer hours than during my Mancino's days...and making *way* more dough (and I don't mean pizza dough!). ☺

SIDE NOTE

My uncle and father continued to run Mancino's for a couple of years without me. Then they pooped out, sold the business, bought a beautiful cottage on the lake, and vowed *never* to get back into the food business. Sixteen-hour days can be rough on the knees.

ACTION ITEMS:

- Ages seven to seventeen, pay attention to your teachers, and listen to your parents. As a thirty-four-year-old goof-off, I wish, more than anything, I could tell my younger self to love education and learn from everyone you can.

- Ages eighteen to twenty-two, don't make the mistake of thinking that you have it all figured out. Embrace education, even if you can't afford to go to college. The Internet has made world-class instruction available to everyone. The time invested now will pay off huge in the future.

- Ages twenty-three to thirty, you have made it to the real world, but make an effort to keep improving your skills every day. My friend and computer programming expert Matt Michaud studies programming languages for at least thirty minutes almost every evening.

- Ages thirty to fifty, make education a vital part of your family time. For better or worse, your kids will become you, so practice good educational discipline! If possible, try homeschooling for a year; you will be amazed at what it teaches *you* and your kids.

- Ages fifty and older, see the quote at the beginning of the chapter! Also, if you believe in the power of education, and there is someone in your life that needs a nudge in the right direction, *give him or her a carrot!* The $500 carrot from my grandfather impacted my life by proving that if I set my mind to a task and gave it all my focus, anything was possible!

HUGE DISCLAIMER

The irony of my thoughts on higher education is this: As I type this chapter, I am on a plane, heading to Vegas, taking my wife to see *O*, the Cirque du Soleil show, for the first time and celebrating the sale of my friend's technology business (for an insane amount of loot, at 168 times EBITDA...unreal). My friend never went to college, but he could teach a Harvard course on hustling and creating the future with his thoughts, actions, and words!

CHAPTER SEVEN

OWNERSHIP

"Freedom begins the moment you realize someone else has been writing your story and it's time you took the pen from his hand and started writing it yourself."

—*Bill Moyers*

So now that you've got your education, I want you to close your eyes and dream big, really, really big, for a minute. Picture the future you are going to make real in your life. Try to go into detail, extreme detail! I'm not going to give you any examples of what to focus on, as I don't want to cloud your vision.

This is an awesome exercise, but, as Jack Canfield was quoted as saying in the first chapter of this book, most people *"cannot see how it could possibly come to them."* If you cannot *see*, you can lose hope, which can brutalize your spirit and cause you to lose faith.

I would suggest that you can see how to get where you are going...so you should never lose hope or faith!

Paths to success are all around you, if you will simply open your eyes and not be afraid to ask questions!

While enjoying a beautiful cabaña on vacation, my good friend was approached by an enterprising young gentleman who took the time to *see and observe* his surroundings. He approached my friend and said, "Excuse me, sir, may I ask you a quick question?"

My friend: "Of course."

The young gentleman: "I just graduated from university and have an awesome job, but how do I get to where *you* are?"

My friend grinned and simply said, "Create something great, and *own* it!"

The young gentleman: "So you're saying I need to become an entrepreneur?"

My friend: "If you can—it worked for me!"

I absolutely loved this exchange for several reasons, and I think there is much to be learned. Here are my observations:

1. The young gentleman was observant enough to notice a happy, successful guy and was *not afraid* to approach him to ask for a bit of

advice. Very cool! I am sick to think of how many times I've had the occasion to solicit a quick nugget of wisdom from someone who has been there and done that, and I let my pride or fear get in the way.

2. The young gentleman mentally connected *"create"* and *"own"* with *entrepreneurship*. Very simple, yet a wise connection! Artists can be entrepreneurs; chefs, athletes, musicians, youth leaders, homeschool mothers, *anyone* can be an entrepreneur if he or she so desires.

3. Own what you create *if you can*. As my friend had invested blood, sweat, and tears into his business for fifteen years before selling it, he knew that not everyone is built to be an entrepreneur. *And that is OK!*

We all have unique goals and life journeys. Not everyone who reads this book is going to write a book or start a business. It takes all kinds in this world, and I thank God for it—how boring if we were all the same!

I was talking to a gentleman by the pool yesterday, and we commented on the *wow* factor of how many *billions* of different ways there are to *do this thing we call life*.

So much diversity...people are beautiful! It appears the Creator is an artist! I believe that we respond to the Creator in what we choose to create with *our* lives...in the little things and the big things! Each one of us is right where we are, *no one* having it all figured out, but all doing the best we can with what we have been given.

The fact is, we are all owners.

We own what we choose to do with each twenty-four-hour block of time that we are blessed with!

ACTION ITEMS:

- Own what you do, all the time! Last month, I had one of my best shopping experiences, ever, at Kohl's. I needed help finding a child's table, and this sweet, grandmotherly lady locked arms with me and led me on my shopping journey though the store. She was so joyful, loved her job, loved the company she worked for, practically loved me. It was so cool! She owned her day, for sure.

- Now that we realize that we should all have an ownership mentality, because each of us is an owner, let's get educated on what that might mean for us. Stretch your ownership abilities outside of your comfort zone. I've recently encouraged my father to take a community college computer class. Enroll in a course on entrepreneurship and see if your creative juices start flowing!

• Don't ever miss another opportunity to ask a potential mentor what advice he or she might have for you. I am so impressed with the young gentleman's humble, yet confident action, "Excuse me, sir, can I ask you a quick question...?" Boy, did I ever learn from him that day!

• Make everything you do a work of art! Sarah and I went to dinner recently and our waiter single-handedly made the experience extraordinary. The food and atmosphere were outstanding, no doubt. We will be back, not because we met the owner (we didn't), but because our waiter loved his life and owned his day, and it made ours!

CHAPTER EIGHT

FLEXIBILITY

"Sometimes, The Next Right Thing might
be to do nothing for a bit."

—*Brandon Ansel*

believe that it will literally change your life if I can convince you to embrace a concept I like to call Flexible Friday.

It is very simple!

> Schedule nothing for yourself on Friday until the day before.

For the past couple of years, I've purposely tried to keep my Fridays flexible. By leaving Fridays open, I'm able to take advantage of unique opportunities that may have presented themselves throughout the week.

In life, things come up, and opportunities present themselves, usually when we least expect it. How many times have you been "too busy" to do The Next Right Thing and strike while the iron is hot?

By leaving yourself some freedom in your work-week, you are able to supercharge your efforts on the most important items that are lining up in your sights!

FLEXIBILITY FOR YOUR TEAM

If you are in a position of leadership, use Flexible Friday to create *insane* employee morale, loyalty, and retention. Depending on your business or industry, you may not be able to give people a full day to be flexible with their time and explore their creative side, but start where you can!

My suggestion is that you at least take a baby step toward letting your team know that you care about them as people and recognize we all have a need for flexibility and creativity in our work. Start with some flexible hours, where folks are encouraged to take some time to expand their horizons, innovate for the company or themselves, and try something new. Your shop will be the shining star of your community, and you will always get the brightest and best job applicants!

So give it a try.

Worst-case scenario, you end up with nothing at all to do on Friday. This rarely happens in the real world, but if it does, here are some things you might consider doing:

- Whittle away at those twelve hundred un-opened e-mails in your inbox.

- Double check your work for the week to ensure that your presentation or follow-up is flawless.

- Ask your dad if he would like to go fishing.

- Get on LinkedIn and make some new connections, or reengage some past relationships. (A LinkedIn recommendation, out of the blue, is sure to brighten someone's day!)

- Surprise your spouse or kids, pick them up from work/school, and take them out to lunch.

- Catch up on a trade journal that's meaningful to you.

- Plot your next business venture.

- Read, pray, meditate, or just enjoy some silence for a little bit. Take ten really deep breaths to clear your mind and enjoy some moments of peace.

- Get that "annual" doctor's exam that seems to only happen for you once every five years.

- See chapter 2 of this book and start your blogging career.

- Call your grandmother and tell her you love her.

- Walk around your city and compliment people on whatever it is about them that seems nice.

- Organize your office and get all that useless *s#!t* off your desk.

- Become a Big Brother or Big Sister! Awesome organization, in my opinion.

ACTION ITEMS:

- See above.

CHAPTER NINE

PARTNERSHIP

"Partnership is the way. Dictatorial
win-lose is so old school."

—*Alanis Morissette*

have been involved in ten successful business ventures over the past ten years, and one very unsuccessful project (more about that later). My business start-up experience has been somewhat all over the map. I've invested, owned, and operated six ventures in the food/restaurant industry. In addition to the hospitality industry, I'm involved in insurance, private equity, consulting, technology, craft beer, and digital media.

The common thread that ties all these ventures together, besides me, is *partnership*. Every business that I've ever invested my time, money, or talents into has been with partners by my side.

In his national best-selling book *The Richest Man Who Ever Lived*, author and entrepreneur

Steven K. Scott titles chapter 6 of his book "The Great Accelerator: The Key to Maximum Success in Minimum Time." The magical business success accelerator that he is referring to is *partnership*. He compares a good partnership, built on mutual trust and respect, as the engine to pursue your dreams at sixty-five miles per hour, as compared with the "snail's pace" of going it on your own.

In the book, Scott describes a partner in the following way:

> A partner or counselor is anyone who can provide needed insight, advice, wisdom, and/or practical help for the effective achievement of a specific project, goal, or dream.

Scott then connects the wisdom of King Solomon to further his belief in partnership:

Without counsel plans are frustrated, but with many counselors they succeed.—Proverbs 15:22

Poverty and shame shall be to him that refuses instruction.—Proverbs 13:18

Every purpose is established by counsel.—Proverbs 20:18

Where no counsel is, the people fail: but in the multitude of counselors there is safety.—Proverbs 11:14

He that walks with wise men shall be wise.—Proverbs 13:20

Two are better than one because they have a good return for their labor. For if either of them falls, the one will lift up his companion.—Ecclesiastes 4:9–10

Though one may be overpowered, two can defend themselves. A cord of three strands is not quickly broken.—Ecclesiastes 4:12

I was fortunate enough to enter into my first partnership in 2001 and was introduced to Scott's book and views on partnership in 2007. It is important to note, though, that there is great risk in partnership too, and you are officially advised to choose your relationships wisely. I have had overwhelming success and great experiences with my partners. There have been challenges, though, mistakes made, that I hope you can learn from!

At the end of chapter 6 in his book, Scott issues the following:

Warning: take care to avoid the wrong partners.

He suggests that we avoid the following characteristics:

1. A lack of integrity.
2. A quick temper or deep-seated anger.
3. Foolishness.
4. Anyone who offers a lot for a little (and I would add, a little for a lot).

5. Excessive flattery.
6. An inclination to gossip and exaggerate.
7. A disregard for rules, regulations, laws, or personal boundaries.

I could opine for hours on the benefits and blessings that I've received, both personally and professionally, from my partnerships. Instead of doing that, I'm going to tell you about my most successful partnership and my least successful partnership. I believe there is much to be gained from both examples.

My Best Partnership

The most important partnership in my life is the one I entered into on July 3, 1999, with a beautiful girl from Monroe, Michigan.

I don't know if "love at first sight" is real or not, but I can honestly say that I experienced something that felt like it in 1995. The first time I brought Sarah Marie Schultz home to meet my parents, my crazy dad literally asked me and this beautiful fifteen-year-old girl, "So when is the wedding?" I thank God that he didn't scare her away!

Anyway, I tell you that story because I believe very strongly that in life, in business, and in love, *you need to trust your gut instincts.* As a seventeen-year-old guy, having fun and loving life, I had absolutely no intention whatsoever of marrying young...quite the opposite. I had it all figured out. I was going to embrace college, get a great job, make my mark on the business world, then, maybe, figure out the family thing.

The fact is, though, my dad was right. As I got to know this gorgeous human specimen, my gut told me rather clearly that if she would have me, I would marry this girl and love her forever. Seventeen years and four babies later, my gut instinct has proven a good guide!

The thing I love most about my wife is that she truly doesn't need me, nor do I need her, but, boy, do we ever complement each other. Opposites attract, as they say, (although it seems more appropriate to say that *complements* attract) and is that ever a good thing, in business and in love. There is secret power in complementary skill sets. This power is multiplied if you take the time to understand and analyze the strengths of your partner and truly appreciate those things that make you different. There have been several times in my marriage that the idiot side of my brain took over and I started to wish that Sarah were more like me. Once clarity set back in, though, I realized what a nightmare it would be to have another "me" in my life. Where I'm weak, she is strong. Where I'm driven, she is laid back. Where I can be narrow minded, a whole world of possibilities is open to her.

My mentor, who happened to be a Top Gun fighter pilot, taught me the power of partnership by telling me that when you are in war, getting ready to jump out of your plane behind enemy lines, the only thing that you care about is who is on your right and who is on your left. The question running through your mind is this: "If I fall down, if I'm hurt, is this person able to pick me up and carry me back to a safe place?"

If I'm going into war, and we all know that business and life involve their share of battles, I want Sarah by my side. I hope she feels the same!

MY WORST PARTNERSHIP EXPERIENCE, THE ONE THAT NEVER HAPPENED

In 2005, my dear cousin and great friend Josh Ansel hired me to help him start a business in our hometown of Monroe, Michigan. Josh was enjoying huge success as a residential and commercial builder and was looking to diversify his business ventures, as he suspected the building boom in Michigan wasn't going to last forever.

I gave my cousin great advice, and the business was up and running quickly, but it eventually failed miserably.

Josh had observed the success of my business and figured that a similar business in Monroe would be successful too. It could have been, but Josh and I failed to recognize the main difference between his business plan and my own. *I had partners in my businesses. He was going in alone.*

A partner with a strong finance background may have helped Josh right the ship earlier and would have picked up on the theft and other issues that were plaguing his venture.

My worst partnership was the one that never happened, and it cost people that I love a great deal of stress and heartache.

Warning: take care to avoid the wrong partners.
(I recognize that this was mentioned earlier, but it's worth repeating!)

As I type this, I'm privy to a phone conversation between my partner and one of his clients. My partner is being absolutely railed by this guy. The verbal lashing is over something that is pretty meaningless in the big picture (unless you believe collateral coverage is the most important aspect of cash-flow-based lending...inside joke).

In business, a client relationship truly becomes a partnership. You become locked at the hip, and your mutual success is entangled together. My partner's stress and frustration level is through the roof every time he has to talk to this client.

Choose Your Partners Wisely

In a vibrant, functioning relationship, each partner tries to give more than he or she gets. That is an incredibly strong foundation for a successful and lasting partnership!

Here are my personal suggestions on traits to avoid in a potential partner/client:

- *Avoid a big ego.* A big ego can suck the life out of a room. It will surely suck the energy out of a relationship.

- *Avoid needy, insecure people.* They will spend all their time overcompensating for their insecurities, which will manifest itself in negativity.

- *Avoid people who overpromise and underdeliver.* This is nothing more than common sense.

You can tell fairly quickly in a relationship if people are going to do what they say they are going to do.

- *Avoid people who procrastinate.* In another section of Scott's book, he writes, "If we fail to take those steps and complete those tasks toward our goal, hope can be put off or, as King Solomon said, deferred. When hope is deferred, it begins to slip away. And guess what happens? As Solomon wrote in Proverbs 13:12, "Hope deferred makes the heart sick: but desire fulfilled is a tree of life." When hope is put off, you lose your emotional energy and your motivation. Your creativity and productivity begin to plummet. You withdraw. Sooner or later, you give up on the vision or dream altogether. Give up too many dreams, and living becomes little more than just getting by. We create the seeds of hope in others by stating or implying commitments. These commitments create a vision. If we fail to fulfill those commitments in a timely manner, we then defer others' hope. They lose their energy and motivation. Moreover, they lose their trust in us. The consequences of deferring hope in others can even lead to the death of a relationship." I tell you this because people who don't do what they say they are going to do can be toxic to a business relationship. There is little worse than hearing, "I'll get it done next week...next month...next year...." As time goes on and that thing doesn't happen, all trust and respect are lost.

Bottom line: If you find yourself in a partnership that isn't working, and you've tried everything in your power to fix it, then The Next Right Thing may be to start taking the steps to exit gracefully while trying to maintain the relationship. There will be extremely difficult conversations, but the rewards will be great for everyone involved. Chances are, the other side of the relationship is probably unhappy and unfulfilled too!

I'll conclude this section on partnership with a reminder that there is incredible strength in knowing that someone has your back.

Seek out partners that add depth, stability, and unique contributions to the plans you have set forth for yourself.

In early 2009 I had decided to launch my own private equity company in Jackson, Michigan. My first step was to find a strong financial partner. I contacted a successful local insurance man who had a reputation of investing his talent and resources into unique business ventures that would benefit his community. I'm exceedingly thankful that he took a risk on me!

When someone takes a risk on you and provides you with the stability or resources that you need in order to fulfill your mission, focus on repaying them a hundredfold! Be the type of partner that you hope the other person will be, and do your best to honor his or her commitment to you, every day. Always give more than you get—I can't stress this enough! Serve your spouse, friends, or partners well! Give generously, as love is best manifested when we sacrifice, and love should be at the root of every good relationship.

ACTION ITEMS:

- In your marriage, friendships, and partnerships, try to always give more than you get. This is a wonderful, selfless way to live life. *I can't stress this enough!*

- Focus on complementary skill sets. Use partnerships to gain access to skills that are not strong for you.

- Get to know the people you are considering doing business with. Take in a baseball game, or get a beer together. Be yourself and let your guard down. Hopefully, they will too, and you can all make an informed decision!

- Always have your partners' back and prop them up! There will, no doubt, be differences among partners. Bicker in the boardroom, though, not in public.

- If you find yourself in a distressed partnership, *look in the mirror!* Triple check, with a humble spirit, to figure out if you might be the problem. For me, more often than not, this is the case. Just ask my wife. ☺

CHAPTER TEN

STRESS

"I promise you nothing is as chaotic as
it seems. Nothing is worth your health.
Nothing is worth poisoning yourself into
stress, anxiety, and fear."

—*Steve Maraboli*

I have purposely tried to keep the pages of this book laser focused on immediate *positive* actions you can take and to highlight concepts to be mindful of when evaluating potential Next Right Things in your life.

Stress is rarely a positive topic of conversation, but I feel strongly that I will have done you, the reader, a disservice if I don't attempt to tackle the cancerous issue of *stress* that I believe is killing the spirit of good, hardworking people all over the world.

PsychologyToday.com defines stress in the following way:

Stress is simply a reaction to a stimulus that disturbs our physical or mental equilibrium. In other words, it's an omnipresent part of life. A stressful event can trigger the "fight-or-flight" response, causing hormones such as adrenaline and cortisol to surge through the body. A little bit of stress, known as "acute stress," can be exciting— it keeps us active and alert. But long-term or "chronic stress" can have detrimental effects on health. You may not be able to control the stressors in your world, but you can alter your reaction to them.

I am so thankful to be able to say that for the past several years, I have been living a life virtually free of chronic stress or anxiety. This has not always been the case, though. I remember an Easter Sunday in 2004 when chronic stress and worry had the muscles in my neck literally seized up and frozen stiff...it was terribly painful, torturous, in fact.

Any countless numbers of outside stimuli or internal triggers inside of us can obviously cause stress. For me, the culprit was always one of two things:

1. An inability to let go of the past. I seemed to always second-guess myself in an endless negative cycle of "Could that have been better?" or "Did I miss an opportunity?"

2. Constant worry about the future. I would put un-
    healthy amounts of mental pressure on myself by
    worrying about things in the future, completely
    out of my control, that might pop up and derail
    my plans. I would stress myself out over things
    that may not even happen. *How stupid is that?*

Constant worry about the past and the future, two totally
separate realities, both completely outside of my control.
It's a wonder that I never had a nervous breakdown.

The Next Right Thing is how I was able to observe
the dysfunction in my life and rid myself of the "stress
monkey" that was constantly on my back, weighing
me down.

If you are living your life with a Next Right Thing
mentality, you cannot obsess over your past choices
in life. If you are focusing on that next right positive
action toward your goals on a regular basis, you feel
confident in the past choices you have made.

The past simply is what it is. It is gone! Learn
from the past, no doubt, but you can never change
it; therefore, it is never worth holding on to and stressing over. Move
on! Intensely focus your attention
on that which you *can* control, that

Let go of the past.

Next Right Thing, which is right with you, right now, right at this moment.

By definition, The Next Right Thing can only exist for you in the present. Not the past, not the future. It is the immediate thing you are focused on, right now, that has all your attention. You will glean nothing from this book if, as you're trying to read it, you're worrying about tomorrow, or next week, or next year.

> Never worry about the future.

The future does not exist right now...it is not real! Those goals, dreams, visions that you have for yourself will come to pass, but you can truly do nothing to affect them except that Next Right Thing! How silly would I have been if I had been worrying about finding a publisher or if anyone would ever enjoy this book *when it wasn't even finished!*

As I've said before, "If you don't know where you are going, how are you going to get there?" Dream big for your future, plot your plan, be excited...*but never stress out or worry about the future.* It will come to pass exactly how and when it's supposed to. A future envisioned with joy will be joyful. A future stressed over will be stressful. Choose joy!

Action Items:

- Alter your reaction to stress. Stress is going to happen, but it has no power over you at all unless you give it power. *Observe* whatever it is that is causing you to feel anxiety. Try to understand why it is there, then *let it go!* Let the stress float past your consciousness as a cloud passes over your head...it's there for a moment, you observe it, and then it is gone, you have moved on.

- Revisit chapter 2 of this book. If something in your life is bothering you, chances are it is unresolved. Resolution leads to action, which leads to peace, health, and wealth.

- Get a good night's sleep! Studies have shown that poor sleep causes stress in your day, which makes it difficult to get good sleep, which causes stress in your day. It's an endless negative cycle if you are not careful. Do whatever it takes to get a good night's sleep!

- Exercise. It is simply great for all aspects of your physical, mental, and emotional well-being.

- Learn to say *no*. Leaving room in your life to be a human means that you may have to pass on certain opportunities or requests. Trying to be all things to all people is the definition of unhealthy stress.

CHAPTER ELEVEN

DEBT

"Life is constantly providing us with new
funds, new resources, even when we are
reduced to immobility. In life's ledger
there is no such thing as frozen assets."

—*Henry Miller*

Unless the genetic pool of the universe has birthed you into an extremely wealthy family whose sole desire in life is to financially support your clearly defined business pursuits, at some point in your financial journey you will require debt.

In my capital markets business, I meet countless would-be entrepreneurs who are seeking capital to fund their dreams. These future business mavens generally fall into one of three categories:

1. The fearful, risk-averse dreamer.
2. The "success is my only option" dreamer.
3. The "success is my only option, but I understand the risks" entrepreneur.

Each of these individuals brings a smile to my face, but only one of them will ever get my time, attention, or access to capital.

The fearful, risk-averse dreamer is probably a brilliant, highly trained engineer who has come up with the next amazing idea while moonlighting from his or her day job. The classic line, the go-to sales pitch, for these folks is always something like "If I only had a million dollars, I would kick it in the ass and make us all rich...." These types are always passionate and love to wave their arms around in the air, but generally lack any type of clearly defined, executable strategy to commercialize their invention or product.

The Next Right Thing for these guys would have been to do the hard work of clearly defining their commercialization, growth, and capital strategies in order to properly articulate how exactly they intend to turn the million dollars they are seeking into bazillions of dollars.

These guys almost always want to give the million-dollar investor 50 percent of their "business" in exchange for the money they seek. When the conversation turns to debt, the fearful, risk-averse dreamer thinks you will be impressed with his or her long dissertations on the debt crisis in America and how debt is evil and dangerous. Obviously it is easy to see right through these folks and conclude that they truly have no idea how they are going to run a business of their own, and they don't truly value their idea, because if they did, they would be trying to secure as much debt as possible so as to keep every percentage point of equity that they can for themselves.

The "success is my only option" dreamer, on the other hand, is the businessperson who is willing to take on any loan at any cost under any terms in order to get the capital he or she needs to fund his or her unstoppable dream. At the end of your first meeting with a person like this, he or she is truly wondering if you have a check in your pocket that you will be making out to his or her business venture on the spot. They are surprised when they leave the office without check in hand.

What I end up wondering is this: If your business idea is so great, and your plans are put together so flawlessly, why are you in my office scrambling for any and every deal that will put cash in your business *yesterday*?

The Next Right Thing for this dreamer would have been to clearly articulate the strengths, weaknesses, opportunities, and threats facing his or her unique business opportunity in order to help a potential capital provider understand the "big picture" of the project or endeavor. To think that your plan is foolproof is to not be a student of history. Great ideas die every day, and for a vast variety of reasons.

In 2012 I met a gentleman who was starting the world's next great network marketing business in the beverage industry. He gave a nice sales pitch, but was shocked that I was not personally writing him a $150,000 check after knowing him for a total of sixty minutes—his deal was that strong, there was no chance for failure (I've heard that one before—☺). I truly appreciate the passion, but raw emotional passion has lost many people a lot of their hard-earned money.

My message to you, if you are that guy:

Stop being an idiot! You are keeping others from helping you be successful by thinking that you have it all figured out!

The "success is my only option, but I understand the risks" entrepreneur is every investor's dream. This future business maven is truly "all in" financially, emotionally, spiritually, mentally, etc. He is going to succeed no matter what, but he is cognizant of the risks inherent in every business deal.

This guy has investigated every debt option available to his particular business model, and is usually seeking help securing that debt or looking for other unique capital options that might be available to help him grow his business and fulfill his destiny.

In early 2012, I was fortunate enough to meet a successful entrepreneur named Conor McCluskey.

Conor had perfected a technology for the successful delivery of video e-mail, no matter which type of device or platform the video was received and played on. Conor had invested every bit of personal financial capital that he had into his business over the previous four years, and was seeking additional growth capital to execute a highly tested and very clearly defined marketing strategy to rapidly add to his installed customer base.

In working with Conor to define the optimal structure for this growth capital, I was highly impressed with the unique debt solution that Conor had already employed during the initial growth phase of his business. Conor had personally guaranteed that debt. This was a significant show of good faith that proved his long-term commitment to the business. We decided together that based on his industry and current balance sheet, there was probably very little additional debt available to him to grow his business, so an equity solution would need to be structured. We then wrestled, quite successfully, over a current valuation of the business that properly valued the work that had already been completed while recognizing that there was still significant work to do, and risk involved, in getting the company to sustainable cash flows.

Conor was able to secure his growth funding, and I invested personally into that deal. Conor seemed to have the perfect blend of DJ Khaled "All I Do Is Win" optimism and Lifehouse "All In" respect and realism. Time will tell how this particular investment plays out, and there is defiantly no guarantee of success, but it would not surprise me one bit if this deal turns out to be the first billion-dollar business venture that I was fortunate enough to get in on early!

Action Items:

Fear not!

- Debt is a tool to be wielded wisely and is powerful enough to command your respect, but you simply *cannot* be afraid of debt if you endeavor to do something great in business.

- Invest your time in studying the proper use of leverage for a business endeavor. Debt is stupid if used to simply buy yourself more junk from the mall, but debt is an amazing money machine if you can figure out how to turn a borrowed dollar into two dollars for yourself!

CHAPTER TWELVE

INSURANCE

"I detest life-insurance agents; they always argue that I shall someday die, which is not so."

—*Stephen Leacock*

About the time that you start acquiring debt, whether it is for a house or a business venture, chances are The Next Right Thing will be to figure out the insurance game. *Insurance is terribly important*, and these next few stories will explain why!

Unfortunately, the insurance industry has a fairly bad reputation. The media are largely to blame for this. You rarely, if ever, hear of the amazing, lifesaving stories of insurance companies stepping up to the plate every day and making good on their promises. Negative headlines get attention, and thus most insurance-related stories revolve around circumstances where, it appears, an insurance company is not taking care of the people it was paid to protect. I understand that this happens, as there are "bad apples" in any industry, but, by and large, insurance is a *really good thing*, and I intend to argue, quite passionately, that you must take the time to understand this amazing tool for "risk transfer" so that you can properly protect yourself, those you love, and those you do business with.

LIFE INSURANCE

My grandfather, Norman Ansel, sold life insurance in Monroe, Michigan, for nearly thirty years. Grandpa Norm had a very strong reputation for being an honest insurance man in an industry that was usually regarded somewhere between snake oil salesmen and bookies.

Over the years, my grandfather protected thousands of families by explaining the value proposition of life insurance: *the ability to protect the lifestyle and financial freedom of the people that you love, in the unlikely and tragic event of your early death.*

The bottom line is this; Life insurance is a complete gift of love. It requires you to sacrifice dollars that you could spend on yourself today in exchange for dollars to be available when you have passed on and are no longer able to provide for your people.

Life insurance is a very hard sell, because *no one* likes to be brought face to face with his or her own mortality. *This is why I have so much respect for individuals in the life insurance industry!* These overworked and underpaid professionals work tirelessly every day to help protect those who are left behind by a tragedy and may not be able to properly fend for themselves.

Bless his heart, Grandpa Norm protected countless numbers of families, but sadly, he never took the time to look in the mirror and properly protect *his* loved ones.

My grandfather had six boys and a beautiful wife who counted on him every day. Like most of us, he must have felt invincible, because in all those years of selling insur-

> I wish someone had sold my grandfather life insurance!

ance, all he ever secured for himself was the $50,000 in life insurance that was sponsored by the company he worked for. *He never sold himself a policy! What the heck?*

Sadly, Grandpa Norm tragically passed away from a heart attack in his midfifties, and Grandma Betty was left with very few financial

> He forgot to drink his own Kool-Aid. ☹

resources to provide for her living expenses over the next thirty-six-plus years (and counting...Grandma is eighty-eight and going strong!).

By the grace of God, Grandma has survived financially over the years. She has struggled but has always been rich in joy, which has spiritually inspired the

> Don't make the mistake my grandpa made!

whole crazy Ansel clan over the years. Though Grandpa Norm completely dropped the ball with regard to his personal life insurance decisions, he did teach all six of his boys the value of hard work, and every one of the Ansel six has gone on to enjoy the success that hard work brings (and has been able to take care of Grandma!).

I heard on the radio recently that the average American spends less than thirty minutes a year on their insurance and retirement planning. *How is that possible?* If the only thing you get from the pages of this book is the prodding to be *intentional* about planning for your future and casting a vision for your family, I will not have let you down! Invest the time today to properly protect your loved ones...literally, *do it today!* Tomorrow can become next week, next month, next year, and it is way easier to do nothing than to do something. The Next Right Thing is to take action on your family's financial planning *today!*

Home Insurance

On Memorial Day 2010, our family was vacationing in Hillsdale, Michigan, when I received a call from my neighbor. It was my neighbors' fourteen-year-old daughter, in fact. She said: "Mr. Ansel, this is not a joke, your house is on fire, and there are ten fire trucks in your yard."

What? How is that possible? Of course it's not a joke! (She wasn't the type of kid to joke about something like that!)

My father and I immediately jumped into the truck and hightailed it back to Jackson County. Sure enough, our beautiful family home, built just four years earlier, was on fire.

The crazy thing is that the month before, I had just received my $1,000 annual insurance bill and had thought to myself, "Geez, I'm never going to use this homeowner's insurance coverage. Maybe I should cut it back and try to save a couple of hundred bucks." (*Yes*, the idiot side of my brain engages way more than I wish it did!)

Thankfully, when I called my insurance agent, he advised me that my coverage was adequate and appropriate...*and was he ever right!* Rebuilding a home and replacing your stuff after a fire is *terribly expensive*.

Six months later, we were back in our beloved home, and it was as good as new! Our insurance company took care of *everything!* They were amazing to work with. They made good on their promises, and I am a walking/talking billboard for them because of it.

MEDICAL INSURANCE

So I will give you all the gory details in the next book I write, but on February 1 of 2013, I broke my hip.

I broke it bad!

Without medical insurance, something as simple as a broken hip can quite literally bankrupt you, or at the very least derail your financial plans. The repair and restoration of my hip, I suspect, will end up costing somewhere between $50,000 and $75,000 when it is all said and done.

Medical care is expensive—insurance is wise!

ACTION ITEMS:

- Set an appointment with a life insurance expert today. Have your policies and coverage reviewed at least every couple of years. Don't make the mistake my grandfather and countless others have made. Get it done today! None of us is guaranteed tomorrow, so do the right thing, and protect those you love. If you do it young, you will be shocked at how affordable insurance actually is. Remember, life insurance is not about you; it is about those people you love the most, who, unfortunately, rarely have a voice in your life insurance decisions. If you live in Michigan, I would call Mel Tejkl at the Walton Agency. She can get you started in the right direction.

- Invest the time to educate yourself and your loved ones about personal financial planning. Don't be the person who only gives these important issues thirty minutes a year!

- For your business, consider key man insurance and buy/sell agreements. As I've said, I love my partners...but that doesn't necessarily mean that I want to be in business with their spouses someday. ☺

- Review your home and auto insurance on a regular basis. Your insurance expert is invaluable in understanding these policies, as they are exceedingly complex. Your agent will be happy to spend the time to educate you, and if not, find a new agent!

- When it comes to health insurance, I'm not going to pretend that I have any idea what the future of it is in America. That said, find a trusted advisor who can help you or your business design the coverage that you need (or may soon be required by law to buy).

CHAPTER THIRTEEN

THE VALUE OF YOUR BRAND

"Your uniqueness is your greatest strength, not how well you emulate others."

—*Simon S. Tam*

quick Wikipedia search will lead you to the following information on brands:

- A brand is often the most valuable asset of a corporation. Brand owners manage their brands carefully to create shareholder value, and brand valuation is an important management technique that ascribes a money value to a brand and allows marketing investment to be managed to maximize shareholder value.

I would argue that your personal brand is the most valuable asset that you will manage in your entire life. Sadly, very few of us were taught anything in school about the incalculable worth of our personal brand, let alone given any tools or suggestions on how to manage it well.

Think about it...how other people perceive you, or what beliefs they hold about you as a human, consumes their vision of who you are. Perception is reality, especially in this type of situation. Every date you ever go on, every sales call you make, every job interview you fumble through, every employee review meeting, every day and in every way, your personal brand is being assessed...whether you like it or not!

This constant assessment of who we are can seem overwhelming, and I understand that. My goal is to get you thinking about it so you can be cognizant of what is going on around you and be proactive in developing what it is that people think about when they think about you!

You, the Sales Professional

The fact is that each and every human on earth is in the sales profession. What do I mean, you might ask? I mean that we are constantly selling ourselves. If you are not aware of this fact, you have been living your life with blinders on.

Could I have landed a girl like Sarah Schultz if I were simply standing around, looking dumb all the time? Fat chance! I didn't realize it at the time, but looking back, oh boy, was I ever selling that blond-haired, blue-eyed beauty! Then I had to sell her parents. I could write a whole book on that sales job. I pity the fast-talking, slick-haired seventeen-year-old who comes around asking to take my little princess Teagan Gabrielle to the movies!

> There is a small sales pitch in almost every human interaction.

Unless you live on an island, you will be interacting with people in this life. You will greatly accelerate your success if you realize the importance of selling yourself first in every situation. It is very basic common sense, but truly worth saying: *people do business with people that they like!*

Who you are, what you stand for, *your brand*, is immeasurably important in every aspect of your life. The achievement of your future goals literally depends on it, so you must manage your brand wisely.

LEVERAGE THE BRAND OF OTHERS

There are all kinds of successes in my life that I am thankful for and proud of. I'm going to list a few below, not to overly toot my own horn but to lay the foundation for the concept of leveraging the brand of others.

- I graduated *summa cum laude* from Spring Arbor University (and it doesn't offend me that you have never heard of this fine institution of higher education).

- I have four fantastic little children who fill my life with joy every day.

- I've owned five successful franchised restaurants.

- I've started several successful companies in the technology and distribution industries with world-class partners.

- I'm married to Wonder Woman!

- I've founded a private equity firm.

- I've partnered with a huge network of independent insurance agencies.

- I have some of the world's greatest friends and family.

I mention all those blessings because they are all a part of my history and the personal brand that shapes others' impressions of me. When I'm looking at a new business venture or raising capital or hiring employees or trying to sell a service, I fully realize that *ultimately I am selling myself.*

So what is this "brand of others" that I claim to leverage so well? Biggby Coffee!

> Not only has our Biggby Coffee franchise been a wonderful financial investment since we opened the shop in Jackson, Michigan, in 2005, it has been an unbelievable reputational investment too.

Biggby Coffee is a Lansing, Michigan-based coffee shop franchise that has literally spent tens of millions of dollars building their brand over the past fifteen years with the goal of becoming the world's best coffee shop. The Big B logo is extremely recognizable all over the state, and if you are a coffee drinker, I suspect there is a 95 percent chance that you have enjoyed a Biggby coffee.

I am consistently amazed that when I am pitching my services to a new potential consulting client, if my resume/background experience (which includes Biggby Coffee) comes up, my franchise ownership ends up dominating the conversation. For some reason, still unknown to me, people find the fact that I have partnered to own a little coffee shop franchise *extremely cool.*

I am convinced that if I had simply owned a "Brandon's Coffee," even if it were the most profitable, yet unknown coffee shop in Michigan, the personal brand value that I receive wouldn't even come close to the brand value I seem to get from my association with Biggby Coffee. They have invested in their brand, yet I have benefited greatly. And no, I do not receive compensation if you go buy a Biggby Coffee franchise tomorrow (even though that might be The Next Right Thing for you!). ☺

ACTION ITEMS:

- Recognize the importance of your personal brand in every aspect of your life, and give your brand the attention it deserves! We are talking about the most valuable asset you have. This is big stuff, and positive brand value doesn't simply happen by chance. This is not about shameless self-promotion. It is about doing everything you do with excellence and passion, and never settling for good enough or almost right.

- Make an investment and bring the coolest little restaurant concept you have ever experienced to your town. Friends and neighbors alike will love you for it, and you will be perceived as a wise, astute businessperson. Ha!

- Make sure you secure your personal domain and have some interesting information displayed there. My website is www.brandonansel.com. I have had several consulting clients mention that they hired me because of info that they found online.

- Be a person! When developing your brand, *authenticity is paramount*. If your brand doesn't represent the "real" you, people will see right through it.

CHAPTER FOURTEEN

EXTRAORDINARY

"All successful employers are stalking men who will do the unusual, men who think, men who attract attention by performing more than is expected of them."

—*Charles Schwab*

Well, it is now 3:30 a.m. on Friday, May 31, 2013, and I am quite literally drinking my own Kool-Aid and practicing what I am preaching at this early hour of the day. The Next Right Thing just forced me to bounce out of bed (against almost every other fiber of my being) to get these thoughts out of my head and into this book.

A quick Google search of the word "extraordinary" yields the following:

1. Very unusual or remarkable.
2. Unusually great.
3. Beyond what is ordinary or usual.
4. Highly exceptional.
5. Going beyond what is usual, regular, or customary.

Who doesn't want to be known as extraordinary? It seems pretty basic, right? "Shoot for the extraordinary, no matter what your passion is in life, and all good things will come your way!"

But how many extraordinary, exceptional things, actions, or people do we actually come into contact within our everyday lives. I would argue, not nearly as many as we should!

For the past several years, I have tried to keep the word "extraordinary" at the top of my mind on a daily basis. This definitely involves trying to do exceptional things throughout the day. More importantly, though, I try to be sensitive to extraordinary things, thoughts, or actions around me so I can record them and learn from them. Two things have been very surprising to me in my journey to observe and demonstrate exceptional behavior:

1. I've observed that there are very few people or organizations attempting to make extraordinary actions or behaviors a part of their normal course of business.
2. When someone is "going beyond" the call of duty, *it sticks out like a sore thumb*, and in a very good way!

A Ray of Sunshine on a Very Dark and Cloudy Day

On February 1, 2013, I severely broke my hip while skiing in Big Sky, Montana, with my brother and several of his friends. Needless to say, it was a very traumatic day for me. Before that day, I had never broken a bone or so much as had a stitch, for that matter. I was far away from my wife and kids. I had no idea how extensive the damage was, but was scared to death because I couldn't move my right leg at all...couldn't even wiggle my toes. I was thankful to be alive, but was terrified at the thought of permanent damage.

I came into contact with no less than fifty highly trained, pleasant, and competent individuals that day. Through the process of trying to get stabilized at the accident site, down the mountain, on the ambulance, to the hospital, thoroughly medically reviewed...you get the picture! *Only one* of those people, though, actually gave me the most important thing that I needed that day, which was extraordinary care and concern. Through all the hustle and bustle, x-rays and exams, and big, scary medical terms, only one person, my anesthesiologist took the time to grab my hand, look me directly in the eyes, and say, "Everything is going to be OK. *I am going to take great care of you!"* That eye contact, the personal touch, and those words were exactly what I needed, and they were extraordinary! Though everyone had given me quality, standard care, no one else, in six hours of medical treatment, had taken the small effort to do the exceptional thing. My anesthesiologist did, thank God, and she was a ray of sunshine for me that day!

RELENTLESS, POSITIVE ACTION

I have come to the simple realization that doing the exceptional thing, or being exceptional, is truly not difficult. It involves making a mental commitment to looking for the common opportunities in your everyday life to do the extraordinary thing...and for no other reason than the fact that the people around you deserve your best. Who doesn't want to have his or her spouse ask how his or her day was and be able to say, "Extraordinary"?

My office in Jackson, Michigan, is one of the few left in the country that has a manually operated elevator. Today that elevator is being retired as an innovative new technology, the automatic elevator, has been installed. ☺ Today is also the last day of work for my friend Cindy. She is retiring after over forty continuous years of operating the elevator in my building. When you ask Cindy how her day is going, she says, "It's had its ups and downs!" She always makes me smile and can brighten my day, and she will be missed! Cindy's career and dedication have been extraordinary in a most unlikely place, especially when measured in smiles.

I recently closed a significant new business deal that involved setting up a new company with a new partner. As we are leaving this very exciting meeting together, my new partner stops me and hands me something. I look down, and I'm holding a solid piece of gold from the US Mint. He then says, "This troy ounce of gold is for you. You can do what you want with it, but I hope you will keep it as a token and memory of our new venture together." Who does that, right? Exceptional people do, and that simple, profound gesture will be long remembered and always appreciated!

The legendary Dave Rice is the operating partner in a company I've invested in, Michigan Agency Partners. Dave seeks to excel in everything he does, and even when knocked down, he comes up swinging hard and always seems to win. When we launched Michigan Agency Partners, our goal was five partner agencies contracted in the first year of business. Dave, of course, decided he wanted to break national records...and has signed up nearly thirty-five agencies as of this date. I had set the bar *way* too low for this extraordinary fellow!

My personal mentor is one of Cleveland, Ohio's, most successful money managers. I have observed, over a period of ten years, that he follows up nearly every meaningful meeting in his life with a handwritten note of appreciation, and often sends a book that he believes will be meaningful to his new friend. That is extraordinary in my opinion.

My business partner, Ken Seneff of Local Logic Media, cooks a hearty breakfast for his staff of programmers and web designers every Monday in their office kitchen. It is a very special thing for me when I get to partake myself, at least once every few months, and observe the magic of the exceptional leadership of the people who make Ken successful. It seems like it is written somewhere that if you want to be great, be a servant of all. That is Ken all the way. He finds his success in helping others achieve their goals and dreams. Ken's customers love him too! His business motto is to give ridiculously more value to his clients than he receives in payment from them. Through technology and innovation, he does it every day!

My wife puts in no less than two hours of prep time every day for the next day's homeschooling lessons for our four children. I am continually amazed by the unique and exciting resources she is able to gather as tools for the home education of our little ones. She takes her educational responsibilities deadly seriously, and her commitment to classical education for our kids is extraordinary!

Ravi Yarid is Hillsdale, Michigan's, premier family doctor and a good friend of mine. Dr. Yarid has a thriving practice and has just built a beautiful new office in the community that he loves and serves. Besides the amazing care that Ravi doles out to his patients, he finds the time to be an awesome husband and father of four. The first time I met Dr. Yarid, he had not one, but *two* exchange students living under his roof. If all that isn't extraordinary enough, I'll tell you this: Ravi is a businessman that I believe is going to change the way people are cared for in America, and maybe around the world.

I have a friend who is going blind and, based on his condition, fully expects to be legally blind by the age of forty-five. I can tell you, the last thing on his mind is "poor me." He has used his situation to his advantage, recognizing that he has to do in twenty productive years what most do in forty: provide a meaningful retirement lifestyle and financial security for his growing family. He has embraced his situation and, through intense focus, is doing exceptional things in business, leadership, and life. His family is blessed, and will never be handicapped or want for anything!

Zingerman's Roadhouse in Ann Arbor, Michigan, is another shining example of excellence at work. The ownership of this restaurant has created a culture where every little detail of the dining experience feels casual, yet exceptional. Here are a few examples:

"I noticed you were considering the barbecued pulled pork, Mr. Ansel, so I brought you a few small samples of the various flavors."

"Oops, I didn't order a cup of chili."

"No worries, Mr. Ansel, I just brought you a little cup, no charge, because I personally love our chili with the burger that you ordered."

(Smart move—I order the chili every time I'm there now!)

These are just a few of the countless personal examples of the extraordinary service that is actually quite common at Zingerman's. I've had no less than twenty dining experiences there, and each of them has been fantastic in its own unique way.

> *When the extraordinary becomes common in your organization or in your life, that is when you know you have won!*

As I reflect on the important people in my life that I've just written about and how they have influenced me and significantly impacted my life journey, it strikes me that the message may simply be this: *endeavor to surround yourself with extraordinary people.*

Action Items:

- Order some nice, professional, personalized stationary and start sending out handwritten notes of appreciation whenever you can.

- Go on Amazon and buy a bunch of copies of a book that has been meaningful to you and give them to people you care about.

- Send your spouse on a weekend away with his/her friends...no special reason and no strings attached! This simple gift will be *stupidly* appreciated!

- Look people in the eyes when you talk to them. It is powerful.

- Remember your trash hauler during the holidays and give him a nice gift card.

- Take your kids to important business meetings with you now and then. They will learn much more in these couple of hours than they will have missed during recess.

- Find a mentor who can challenge you and stretch you as a person.

- Seek out people you are impressed with, and find a way to positively impact their life.

- Make a list of business contacts you would like to reengage with, and start setting appointments, even if the calls make you uncomfortable.

- Learn one new life skill every six months. Extraordinary individuals seem to have a strong commitment to lifelong learning!

- Write a book. It is easier than you think, and your kids will enjoy reading it someday. ☺

CHAPTER FIFTEEN

AVAILABILITY

"Sometimes half the battle in making a
sale is simply showing up."

—*Wise Sales Proverb*

n a business setting, in the digital, real-time, connected age that we live in, the service aspect that I seem to value most, as a consumer, is *availability!*

In the era of cell phones, back-up cell phones, Wi-Fi, iPads, laptops, 4G, Google Voice, e-mails, text messages, FaceTime, call forwarding, and the like, it is a mortal sin to not be available when your customer is ready to make a deal!

Exceptional service is *paramount* in the business world these days, because it is simply too easy for your customer to search out your competitor on his or her smartphone.

Don't get me wrong, relationships are still the cornerstone of any business dealing, but I'm often observing that service and availability are becoming almost as important as relationships in getting a deal done.

My doctor recently suggested a hot tub might be just what I need to help ease the pain of my broken hip. I was, obviously, over the moon, as I had been looking for a nonnarcotic pain management solution, and heat therapy sounded perfect!

I took the day off of work, and my wife and I set to the task of having a therapeutic hot tub delivered to our home as soon as possible.

Our first call was based on a relationship that we have, through our church, with a local family that owns a very nice hot tub showroom. They were going to get our business purely on relationship, but, unfortunately for them, that did not work out.

Here is why...

When I called their store, a very friendly gal answered the phone. The conversation went something like this:

ME: "Hi, Brandon Ansel calling for Joel about buying a hot tub today. Is he around?"

GAL: "I'm sorry, Joel is in and out today. He is very busy with the new building."

ME: "I understand. Do you expect him back soon? I've taken the day off and am ready to get a deal done!"

GAL: "No, I'm not sure exactly when to expect him back, but can I take a message and have him call you?"

ME: "Sure, but would you please try to get the message to him ASAP? I rarely take time off for things like this, and I'm ready to make a hot tub purchase."

GAL: "OK, I'll do my best."

Not a bad conversation, but not an exceptional one either. She missed a perfect opportunity to seal a relationship sale for her boss. It would have been *so* easy for this nice gal to offer to give me Joel's cell phone number. I would have called him, or probably sent him a text, about my interest and timing. He then could have easily responded and sealed the relationship, thus winning himself the time to be available later in the day. Because I had no clear path with regard to timing or communication with Joel, I was quickly on to the next option. Like most impatient Americans, when I want something, I want it *now*.

> Be available! It can be as simple as a text message saying you will be back with me in a couple of hours. Based on relationship, I would have, no doubt, given Joel that opportunity, and he would have gotten the sale.

So my next option was a very high-end spa retailer about thirty minutes from my home. Sarah and I quickly Googled them, and we confirmed that they were open and that they had plenty of hot tubs on site to choose from.

This place was awesome! Tons of floor models to preview, and our sales associate was friendly, pleasant, and knowledgeable. They were on the high side of our budget, but I was ready to make a deal. I now thought, for sure, that this would be the company to get my business that day.

Everything was going perfect, and I made a very fair offer on a very high-end hot tub (which I figured had great margins baked in for the retailer). The transaction derailed, though, when no one was *available* to make a deal. My sales associate was only authorized to sell for sticker price. *Profitable sale lost, again, due to lack of availability.*

How easy would it have been for the owners of that establishment to train their people in the art of the close and to empower them to make a deal within an acceptable range of financial possibilities? This is so easy, yet I observe so many businesses that lose so many sales because they either don't train or don't trust their people, or they don't have a decision maker available all the time.

Sarah and I were pretty disappointed, but then she remembered that there used to be another hot tub shop in the Michigan Center

> No hot tub for us. ☹

area, Blue Water Pool and Spa of Michigan. She Googled them and, sure enough, they were still in business thirteen years after selling us our first hot tub, shortly after we had gotten married and bought our first home.

> Why had they not continued to market to us? Our e-mail address hadn't changed! That is for another book or another chapter. In any business, you can never stop marketing to your database!

Sure enough, we stopped at the store in Michigan Center and the showroom looked great. The owner was *available*, she remembered us after thirteen years (extraordinary), and she was ready to make a deal. Suffice it to say, I'm typing this as her husband and his crew are installing my new therapeutic hot tub!

Availability wins the day...and makes the profitable sale! Why every business doesn't utilize every avenue and technology possible to be available when their customers are ready to buy, I will never understand...but I can promise that if you do embrace availability, you will dominate your industry!

ACTION ITEMS:

- Embrace availability! Utilize every form of technology that you reasonably can to make it easy for your customers or potential customers to cement a relational touch point with you.

- Texting has become a powerful and preferred communication platform for business. I believe it is currently the best way to create very soft touch points with your circle of influence. Even if you can't connect with someone right away, send him or her a quick text to show that you care. This is powerful, easy, commonsense stuff!

- Teach your people how to make a freaking deal, and empower them to get it done. Making a sale is never easy, but when someone walks in your door with cash, don't miss out because you were too lazy to train your sales professionals on how to negotiate a profitable deal! Information and pricing are everywhere, and your competition is worldwide now that the world is flat. The businesspeople that win will be the ones who properly train and empower their people to make deals.

- The Next Right Thing is to encourage your assistant or staff to give out your cell phone number to prospects. You may have to deal with a pain-in-the-butt customer every now and then, but the enhanced relational value will far outweigh the burden of the occasional crazy!

- Log in to your LinkedIn account immediately, and make sure that your business circle has access to all of your contact information. List your cell number right next to your name. What's the worst thing that can happen...you get calls from prospects?

CHAPTER SIXTEEN

LEADERSHIP

"One can never consent to creep when
one feels an impulse to soar."

—Helen Keller

I t is almost embarrassing to try to write anything meaningful for you on the topic of leadership. There is simply *so much* good material out there to help each of us become better and more effective leaders, I just don't know if anything new can be said.

What I am going to try to give you, though, are those thoughts, ideas, and concepts about leadership that I've observed and tried to demonstrate, or that simply resonate deeply in my soul.

I'll start with what resonates most deeply.

> A leader is most effective when serving those people he is trying to lead.

As I mentioned earlier, in 2003 my partner and I opened our first franchised restaurant concept in Jackson, Michigan. By 2005, we had five franchised restaurants opened and operating. We had one hundred employees and were enjoying nice success for a couple of young guys in their midtwenties (in no small part thanks to the trust and support of Charles W. Morgan, my partner's father, our financial backer).

When we opened our first store, our franchise representative told us that our biggest headache in the restaurant business was going to be employee turnover. He was constantly telling us stories about how unreliable restaurant workers were. His favorites were the "Three-Month Rule" and the "PlayStation Rule."

- Most every person you hire will quit or be fired within the first three months of employment.

- Most every male high school student will quit his job once he has saved up enough money for a new PlayStation.

Neither rule proved true for us, and we were, and continue to be, amazingly blessed with long-term and loyal employees, several of whom have been with us for many, many years!

I have had the high honor of deep, candid conversations with several of our key, long-term people and have been able to ask, "What has made you stick around so long?" One gal told me she has stayed because we always seemed to treat her like the most important person in the world. When told that, I said something like, "We did? That's great, but what do you mean?" She went on to explain that in all the years she had worked for us, we had never denied her a vacation request or complained if she needed time off for her family...we always did our best to accommodate, even if it meant one of us working the shift ourselves. Apparently she had worked at a couple of places where missing a shift for a family emergency meant immediate termination.

I am humbled by that story, because the fact is that *she* is the most important person in *her* world, and by the grace of God, Matt and I always seemed to understand that fact and tried to serve our people accordingly. We covered many a weekend shift in our early days as pizza makers because of school dances or sick kids. It seems crazy to me that people have ever been reprimanded due to sick kids!

Life happens for each and every one of us. Ninety-five percent of the time, our employees perform exactly how we need them to perform, and *we win* because of their hard work and effort. During those 5 percent times when life happens and they need us to have their back, you better believe we are going to try our best to serve them well.

From 2007 to 2009 I worked for a small private equity firm in Cleveland, Ohio. We had about eighty-five employees spread out in eight offices around the country. I was fortunate enough to be the youngest member of our fifteen-person leadership team. The leadership team had a call monthly, met together in person every six months, and each of us would meet individually with the CEO about every thirty days.

> The job of a leader is to destroy all "barriers to success" that his/her team encounters.

I always enjoyed our calls and group meetings, but the one-on-one time with the CEO was always powerful and inspiring for me. Our company had a very clearly defined mission and vision. The simple fact was that the CEO ran the entire company by asking each member of his leadership team, every month, "What can I do to help you break down any barriers to success you are facing?" This question came with the implied understanding that we were each working diligently toward our common mission and vision for the future of the company. *And then he destroyed the barrier, whatever it was!*

Of course, I'm making it seem quite a bit simpler than it actually is in real life. The point is that each member of the leadership team knew, without doubt, that our boss had our back and would do anything in his power to help us be successful. We all win together!

> A leader sees in others the potential that they might not yet see in themselves.

In 2011 I had the good fortune of interviewing a young guy, twenty-four years old, from JP Morgan Chase, with the goal of hiring him and teaching him the capital markets business.

I am not in any way claiming to be a great leader; sometimes it's better to be lucky than good. I can confidently say, though, that I saw a future leader in this young guy that he probably didn't yet see in himself.

He most definitely showed ambition and clearly had very big goals and dreams for his life, but one person can only do so much. What I saw, and what has been developing over the past two-and-a-half years as we continue to work together, is someone who can achieve even bigger goals by casting a vision, leading a team, and helping others become successful.

The best part about this young guy is that in thirty months of working together, I've not once had to "manage" him. He is highly self-motivated and desires nothing more than to do something significant with his life. I've often described him to others as "someone who is going to be *way* better than me in an industry that I think I'm pretty damn good in." As the famous author Jim Collins is often quoted saying, "Get the right people on the bus, then figure out where to go."

Love well.

I can sum up my thoughts on leadership by stating my belief that a great leader will be known for loving his or her people well. By loving and respecting those people who work for you, you acknowledge the divine spark of possibility that they actually are...and who doesn't want to feel like the most important person in the world!

Action Items:

- Study servant leadership. Google "servant leadership"—there is tons of great material out there.

- Take good care of yourself! It is nearly impossible to become a leader of people, if it's perceived that you can't take care of yourself.

- Invest your time in "vision casting." This is critical for a business and is great for a family too! Sarah and I spend time every year to clearly define what we want the next one, five, and ten years to look like for our family. Remember, "Where there is no vision, the people perish" (Proverbs 29:18).

- Great leaders speak their plans clearly and simply. Complexity is the enemy of success. Practice simplicity in your personal and business dealings.

- Practice makes perfect, and leadership is *influence*; thus, *you* are a leader, whether you realize it or not, because we all exert influence every day. Make a conscious effort to positively influence at least one person every day. Hold yourself accountable by asking your spouse to ask you, "Whom did you influence today?"

CHAPTER SEVENTEEN

COMMUNICATION

"I find it unusual that it is more socially acceptable to complain about what you have than it is to ask for what you want."

—*Phil Lout*

As a business consultant, I have had the unique opportunity to "peek under the covers" of well over one hundred family-owned businesses over the past ten years. I'm often brought in to help a company more clearly define a growth strategy, develop a strategic plan, or assist in capital planning. More often than not, though, I end up consulting with ownership and management as to their internal communication issues. Every business has them!

The reason for this is simple. Human communication is *extremely* complex.

Let's look at the example of the typical, successful, family-owned business with fifty employees. In this example, let's say that seven of those employees are a part of the management team. Then let's throw in a couple of outside consultants—trusted advisors, we will call them—that are also part of the team.

You now have fifty-two completely different communication styles at play. Not to mention personalities, belief systems, past experiences, world views, hopes, dreams, insecurities, fears, etc.

Now consider the fact that each of these individuals is living in his or her own unique bubble of perception. It is obvious and easy to see how well-intended communication can go terribly wrong.

Unfortunately, I have yet to find a magic bullet of communication strategy to solve the complex issues that we all encounter in human interaction. That said, I am not afraid to offer you the following seven tips on how to be a better communicator in all aspects of your life, specifically when it involves dealing with conflict. (No one needs any communication advice during a love fest!)

1. State your opinions as simply and clearly as possible.
2. Understand intentions. When communicating in a situation where there is discourse and disagreement, get everyone involved to agree that each individual enters the conversation

as a good person with good intentions as to the outcome of the disagreement.

3. Don't ever be passive/aggressive. Passive/aggressive communication is easily observed and never well received. It is a very weak form of communication that will always make you look bad.

4. Listen well, make eye contact, and then ask appropriate questions. Truly seek to understand the other side of a disagreement.

5. I realize that it completely goes against human nature, but *you do not always have to be right!* This has been a very tough one for me to master, but, amazingly, I've found there is huge strength in gracefully being wrong sometimes.

6. Try hard to enter the other person's "bubble of perception." More often than not, it is perception that clouds communication. The only way I've found to overcome this huge hurdle is to try to view a situation through the eyes of others.

7. Communicate respectfully at all times! The quickest way to create an enemy for life is to disrespect someone in the presence of their peers.

I hope you will practice these seven tips and make them a part of all your critical conversations. One of my greatest joys in business is when I can help people solve problems or conflicts through effective communication.

ACTION ITEMS:

- Buy the book *The 5 Love Languages*, by Gary Chapman. Read the book twice. If the information in Gary's book doesn't greatly enhance your marriage, friendships, and business relationships, I will eat my shirt!

- See the seven tips above!

CHAPTER EIGHTEEN

FORGIVENESS

"Revenge is easy, forgiveness is difficult...
It is always the right thing, but boy,
is it ever difficult."

—*Brandon Ansel (unless someone else said it first)* ☺

nless you have become the Jedi master of human communication and have never pissed anyone off, there is a very big chance you will have to figure out forgiveness in this life... both receiving forgiveness and being able to forgive.

This is a tough one for me, a very tough one. When someone wrongs me, my genetic disposition is to immediately try to figure out how to get him or her back...an eye for an eye, as they say.

I know that you have been there too and know exactly what I am talking about!

The problem with this base instinct is that it can create an endless cycle of "I'm going to get you back!" Your neighbors who wronged you probably felt wronged themselves, and now that you have gotten them back, they will be keeping their eyes open for how to get you back. Endless negativity—why are we wired this way?

I had to practice what I preach on forgiveness this week, and I'll tell you what, it was a tough pill to swallow!

My neighbor of seven years, whom I truly love, had the police called to my house this week.

What, pray tell, was the criminal enterprise that prompted my generally good-natured neighbor to sic the heat on me? *Poultry!*

As I've mentioned, we are a homeschooling family, for all sorts of reasons. One important reason is that we can teach our children unique life skills that might not be available in the traditional educational setting. To that end, in order to teach our four little inquiring minds about business and self-sufficiency, we engaged my grandfather, a farmer, to build us a chicken coop and teach us the joy of raising chickens. Our goal was to teach the kids responsibility (caring for the pet chickens) and business (buying the chicken feed and setting up an organic "egg sale" stand).

Half of our educational plan was immediately crushed when my wife called the township we live in to make sure we were not breaking any rules. She was told that we were not zoned for agricultural purposes, which meant, we believed, we could not raise chickens for commercial purposes...only as our children's pets.

Sad as we were about the missed business opportunity, our kids were still overjoyed at the thrill of raising, loving, and getting sustenance (eggs) from their pet chickens. We purposely did not purchase any roosters, as we did not want to disturb our neighbors!

When the chicken coop was being installed, we talked to our closest neighbor—we will call him Bill—and told him the kids are excited to give him and his wife fresh eggs, probably in six months. He didn't say much, but certainly didn't voice any concern at that time. Why would he? We have been great neighbors; we are friendly, quiet, we keep our property and landscaping beautiful, and the chicken coop was first class, even custom landscaped!

Four weeks later, the baby chickens were delivered, and the kids were having a blast, feeding them, watering them, even cleaning the coop every other day. They worked hard and never complained. I was so proud!

Strangely, though, Bill was not proud. About a month into our chicken adventure, Bill walks over to our property while my wife is outside with the children and tells Sarah something like this:

"I do not like chickens. Actually, I hate them!"

Sarah was confused and felt uncomfortable and intimidated. She was not able to tell me how the rest of the conversation went, as she was rattled, but suffice it to say, it did not go well.

Our neighbor didn't tell us why exactly he hates chickens, but before you know it, the cops are knocking on my door.

The police officer was extremely nice, even apologetic for having to stop by, but the bottom line is that my neighbor called and complained about the chickens. I explained that they were pets, and we were not going to use them for commercial or agricultural purposes as originally intended.

The officer took the time to meet our chickens, and complimented us on the beautiful coop. She let us know that we would be getting a letter from the township stating that we may not be able to keep the chickens. She encouraged us to review the township ordinances, which we did. It did not state anywhere that we could find what pets are and are not allowed in a residential area.

Quite candidly, our little yapping dog is *way* more annoying than our chickens...they don't make a peep!

The point of this story is that as I observed the situation, everything inside me wanted to get back at this neighbor, whom I felt was trying to sabotage my children's educational experience...*and I had some data to support my revenge!*

Being forced to now become an expert in local zoning ordinances, I found at least two glaring violations that my neighbor commits on a consistent basis...and they both revolve around garage sales.

Local ordinances allow only one garage or yard sale every ninety days, for *personal* property.

My neighbor, for years, has had more than one huge garage sale every summer. You cannot imagine how many people he draws in for these massive sales! In addition, he has been known to do "sales for hire" where he will sell other peoples estates for a percentage of the sales. This is also against the local ordinance, as the township only allows a garage or yard sale for *your personal property*, not for profit.

Yeah, I can get my revenge. If he wants us to kill our pet chickens, I will put a stop to his beloved garage sales!

And then I looked in the mirror and everything changed!

What I saw was a guy who desperately needs for-giveness more than most. I can be short and insensi-tive, I am a steamroller in a business setting, and I've been known to hurt those that I love the most. The fact is that I screw up all the time, but I always want forgiveness. Everyone does.

The bottom line is that I'm going to forget about revenge and learn to forgive Bill...whether we have to get rid of our pet chickens or not.

Forgiveness is simply the right thing to do, every chance we get! Even when we feel right, and it is *hard*, we still need to forgive!

I'm not sure if my relationship with Bill will ever get back to where it was. I'm confident, though, that revenge is not the right answer, even if, for a time, it may have felt good. I'm thankful that I didn't follow my *feelings* and make an enemy, **because feelings come and go**.

Forgiveness goes against our nature; you might say it is divinely inspired.

ACTION ITEMS:

- Every chance you get to do something "divinely inspired," *do it*. Your life will be better for it!

- Drink some "grace juice" every morning! Put your "grace goggles" on, every day, and look for opportunities to extend grace to the people in your life. Hopefully grace will be there for you if you ever need it!

- Fight that instinct to "get even" every chance you get. Revenge creates enemies, and who wants enemies?

- In your family, friendships, or at work, be generous with forgiveness. Don't be that person who is always "keeping score" of rights and wrongs. If you try to do this, everyone loses.

- When you have some free time, read your local zoning ordinances...it may keep you out of trouble!

Humility

"True humility is not thinking less of yourself, it is thinking of yourself less."

—*C. S. Lewis*

recognize that a certain amount of swagger is important, and probably necessary, if you endeavor to do something significant with your life. (Shoot, I actually have a rap name, White Smoke, for when I decide to crush the local karaoke scene with my unique blend of hardcore, yet socially conscious hip-hop music.) If you have any amount of positive self-image, you probably have a deep down belief that you are living the best life you possibly can. Living your best life is pretty cool, no doubt! Letting arrogance creep into your personality, though, is like asking the universe to trip you over your own shoelaces.

The fact remains that we generally don't consider the importance of humility enough in our everyday lives. If we are not careful, this can become even more true, and humility becomes even harder to practice as we begin to enjoy success.

My grandfather's favorite quip is, "It's hard to be humble when you are perfect in every way." That line always gets chuckles and smiles, but I can see in my life, and in others, there is something that we hold on to in jokes like this. As I alluded to in the previous chapter, we humans *despise* being wrong...we simply want to live in the la-la land of Oz where we are great and powerful. The facades that we hold tightly to, and that seem so important to us, are actually killing out spirit. Your *ego* is not your friend.

There is peace in not having all the answers.

There is strength in asking for help.

There is salvation in seeking forgiveness.

There is power in letting others see us for who we really are.

No one has taught me these truths more than my brother. Brock Ansel is one of the most universally loved people that I know. Rarely has Brock had a meaningful conversation that didn't lead to a friendship. Brock has the most interesting blend of humility and confidence that I've ever observed in a person. He is who he is, all the time. No pretense, no filter, no mask, just Brock.

Candidly, I used to believe that Brock's personality was a strange blend of youthful ignorance and an egoless ego. (Whatever an egoless ego is.)

I realize now, after countless years of people simply responding to him with love and joy, that Brock's ability to always be exactly who he is *is* how he expresses humility.

He doesn't have the silly pride issues that most of us have. He never tries to be all things to all people. He doesn't have to *try* anything at all. He is Brock to everyone...it is what it is. *It is a good way to live.* He is a truly joyful specimen who blesses the lives of those lucky enough to call him a friend.

The message I want to convey is this: *Don't take yourself too seriously.*

The following are a few more of my favorite insights on humility:

- "There is nothing noble in being superior to your fellow man; true nobility is being superior to your former self."—Ernest Hemingway

- "True humility does not know that it is humble. If it did, it would be proud from the contemplation of so fine a virtue."—Martin Luther

- "I have been driven many times upon my knees by the overwhelming conviction that I had nowhere else to go. My own wisdom and that of all about me seemed insufficient for that day."—Abraham Lincoln

- "The only thing I know for sure is that I am wrong."—Wise proverb

- "Everybody is wrong about everything, just about all the time."—Chuck Klosterman

ACTION ITEMS:

- Don't take yourself too seriously!

- Embrace your inner swagger and you will have a blast in life, but check your ego at the door!

- Exude competence, not arrogance.

- Have strength, and be the first person to express an opinion. Do this with a humble spirit and be open to the fact that others might offer a more valid solution.

- Being real and vulnerable with people makes a powerful impact and speeds up trust. I tell most all my consulting clients that I believe I can add significant value to their business, but am driven by a healthy fear of never wanting to let them down.

- As my friend Ric says, don't read your own headlines!

CHAPTER TWENTY

LOVE GENEROUSLY

"Christmas, my child, is love in action. Every time we love, every time we give, it's Christmas."

—*Dale Evans Rogers*

"It's not given to people to judge what's right or wrong. People have eternally been mistaken and will be mistaken, and in nothing more than in what they consider right and wrong."

—*Leo Tolstoy*

t this point, I hope you are coming to the realization that The Next Right Thing, when executed relentlessly, is like a legal and healthy performance-enhancing drug for your brain!

In this chapter, I hope to convince you to use your new power for good.

I have a close friend from Grand Rapids, Michigan, who is a high-end estate-planning money manager. The very first time I met this gentleman, we'll call him "Berke," I observed him living his life and conducting his business with a Next Right Thing mentality.

The unique thing about Berke, though, is that his Next Right Thing almost always includes helping others be successful in their personal or professional endeavors. He is constantly investing his time, talent, and relationships into helping those people whom he cares about and believes in. He is also an expert at leveraging relational capital by matching up skill sets in his network so that sometimes 2 + 2 can equal 10. Together everyone wins!

Berke lives by the mantra "Always make your contribution greater than your reward…otherwise the rewards start to disappear."

Berke loves generously, all the time, with no expectation or ulterior motive. This is very natural for him and seems to come from his personal faith and general enthusiasm for life. Consequently, almost everyone who meets Berke wants to figure out how to do business with him. Success is a foregone conclusion, and everyone wins.

Do well by doing good! Life is not a zero-sum game…a win for you does not mean that someone else has to lose. If you love well, you will find situations where everyone wins.

I state the above, so you can be mindful of what you believe in your core. If you believe that there is room for everyone at the top, you will love selflessly and stand out in the crowd. If you believe that the only way for you to win is to

> Beliefs trump everything when it comes to people and to business.

rig the system in your favor, you will be just like every-one else who is ruled by his or her basic instincts, and be known as a small-minded, shady businessperson.

I find that a judgmental, narrow-minded attitude will get you nowhere in business, or in any relationship, for that matter.

> Judge nothing. Observe everything.

When you judge something, you stuff it into a very narrow little crevice in your brain. There is the possibility that your brain will wedge it there tightly and hold on to that judgment for all eternity. This may or may not be a good thing. Observation is the better route!

When you observe something without casting judgment on it, you leave yourself and that which you are observing in a constant state of freedom. A constant state of freedom allows room for all involved to grow, and breathe, and change, and become better.

When I first started pitching my private equity initiatives to successful business leaders in Jackson, I was introduced to a gentleman in the health care industry. The gentleman agreed to meet with me at the suggestion of a friend. I was excited about the meeting, but unfortunately, it didn't go well at all. Within five minutes, the gentleman had judged me as unworthy, chewed me up, and spit me out. I had never had that happen before...what an unsettling experience. The interaction shook me, but it didn't slow me down at all. I have gone on to enjoy significant success in my venture, and those involved have done extremely well. The gentleman I met with has not lost any sleep over our encounter either; all he lost was five minutes of his very busy day.

I learned an extremely valuable lesson that day, and it has guided most every business interaction that I've had since then. *I will not judge people and put them into a box.*

In the spirit of loving generously, I enter every meeting I am blessed with, with a truly open mind, observing, looking for opportunities. If something doesn't resonate with me right away, I don't write it off, I store it up and allow it to grow, and breathe, and change, and become better.

I know that I can learn something from, and hopefully give something to, every single person that I meet. Observe everything, and grab on quickly to those things that sit well in your soul. Keep everything else in a state of freedom, and watch it, and be ready to add value if and when the time becomes right!

Reference point: I completely understand the difficulty of trying to "judge nothing" in a world where we are constantly required to use our judgment each moment of the day...is it safe to cross the street...is that bread moldy? There is a huge difference between using good judgment and casting judgment. One brings life and safety to a world of chaos, while casting judgment is nothing but harmful and destructive.

ACTION ITEMS:

- Hug a lot, and be cautious of people who don't enjoy a nice hug every now and then!

- The key to being able to love generously is to be secure in who you are and to be thankful for the gifts and talents that you have been blessed with. Current limitations are just future strengths to be learned and are never anything to be ashamed of! You can't love others if you don't first love yourself.

- If you ever find yourself without lunch plans on your calendar, choose anyone, take him or her to lunch, and ask what you can do to help him or her be successful...no strings attached.

- If you ever feel the need to cast judgment, look in the mirror first. It is better to judge yourself in a constant, positive self-evaluation. Am I on track to achieve my personal and family goals? Am I doing The Next Right Thing on a consistent basis? Am I practicing proper dental hygiene?

- Get involved in a worthwhile charitable organization. Show your kids the importance of community involvement. Give back with your time and talents. There is no better way to love generously than to sacrifice for the greater good.

CHAPTER TWENTY ONE

BE AN OPTIMIST

"Work is either fun or drudgery. It depends on your attitude. I like fun."

—*Colleen C. Barrett*

Generally, most everyone I meet would consider himself or herself to be a positive person. I've met a few, though not many, who are self-proclaimed pessimists. Though the vast majority of us believe we are feeling good throughout the day, the data suggests otherwise.

My wife and I recently hosted a parenting seminar that was put on by my friend Greg Gallagher. Greg is the founder and CEO of Solutions 2 Wellbeing and Recovery Technologies. Greg's passion for over thirty years has been to help people profoundly improve their lives with minimal emotional pain, using the most effective and expedient treatment approaches available. Greg truly cares about people and their families.

During the presentation, Greg referenced research that concluded the average human adult brain processes *over forty thousand negative thoughts per day.* This was mind blowing to me at first, but then I did two things that seemed to support Greg's statement.

1. I consider myself an extremely positive person, so as a test I started paying close attention to the fleeting thoughts that pass through my mind on a daily basis, and was startled. "You are going bald." "You don't work out enough." "You don't spend enough time with your kids." "You take on too much risk." "You're fat." "You have a zit." "Your nose is big." You get the picture, I'm sure. Now 99 percent of these thoughts simply come and go and are not even noticed. Scary to me was that they are there, and are most likely effecting my subconscious beliefs...beliefs about myself and beliefs about the world around me.

2. I Googled it and, sure enough, there was all sorts of information available to sift through on the subconscious negativity that presumably lurks in all of us.

So what do you do with information like this? Do you hide under a rock? Do you pop in your earphones and put your inspirational playlist on auto-repeat?

Do you buy self-help books that will tell you how good you are?

My conclusion, and my advice to you, is that you fight the "negativity beast" in yourself and help fight it in other people every chance you get! This was the only course of action that made any sense to me. Be lavish with praise every chance that you get. Look for the opportunities to pass out a kind word to others. Focus on the unique beautifulness that is you, and be thankful for that beauty all the time. Your perception of the world around you is strongly influenced by your beliefs. Your beliefs are developed through your life experiences. *Engage in experiences that will bring positivity to your life!* Join a service organization; Kiwanis does amazing things to make the world a better place. Attend a church and meet new people. Volunteer at a children's hospital and bring joy, hope, and optimism to these kids in need. You will be so blessed!

Action Items:

- Test this negativity thing for yourself. I sincerely hope that these forty thousand negative subconscious thoughts don't exist for you. If they do, though, observe them so you can fight to get rid of them by focusing on the positive. Beauty and joy are truly inside you, and all around you, all the time.

- Surround yourself with positive people!

- When other people want to add positive people to their life, be the first person that they think of!

- Give of yourself. We are all so interconnected, and by giving, I can promise, you will be blessed beyond measure!

- If you need some help, call Greg Gallagher. His life's work is helping people overcome negativity and find well-being!

Chapter Twenty Two

Give More Than You Get

"Goodness is the only
investment that never fails."

—*Henry David Thoreau*

ive more than you get, and never stop doing The Next Right Things!

Action Items:

- Read the book *The Go Giver*, by Bob Burg and John David Mann.

- Put the five *Go Giver* laws of stratospheric success into action!

Epilogue

It is not one big thing that significantly changes your world. It is the small, incremental right things that you keep doing, on a consistent basis, that add up to an amazing reality.

Made in the USA
Charleston, SC
08 March 2014